W9-DDT-442

You, Your Child and Drugs

by the staff of
THE CHILD STUDY ASSOCIATION OF AMERICA
WEL-MET INCORPORATED

The Child Study Press

*The publication of this book has been
made possible through the support of the
Helena Rubinstein Foundation, Inc.*

Copyright © 1971 by
The Child Study Association of America, Inc.

Printed in the United States of America
All Rights Reserved

Standard Book Number: 87183-238-0
Library of Congress Catalog Card Number: 77-122013

Designed by Roland A. Moch

Contents

The Need
For New
Perspectives

1

"Drug epidemic," "youth culture," "generation gap": these are only a few of the phrases that bombard parents as they try to understand the drug problem and figure out how they can protect their children from the dangers it poses. A steady stream of articles, books and newspaper stories has made parents more knowledgeable about drugs but it has exacted a high price of us: vastly increased anxiety, guilt and a sense of helplessness.

On the one hand we are made to feel that it is mostly our fault if our children have problems with drugs—or anything else. On the other hand we are told that we are so alienated from the younger generation that we cannot hope to be influential in their lives. Other contradictions, as well as some misinformation, pervade the popular literature on drugs. Catchwords and slogans often substitute for sensible thinking. Hysteria mounts. In all this turmoil, parents are sorely in need of new perspectives. We need to know how we, our children and society share the responsibility for the drug problem and can work together to find solutions.

WHAT CAN PARENTS DO?

There is no magic recipe for keeping children from experimenting with drugs or whatever dangers are abroad in their environment. There are no instant solutions for so vast a social problem as drug abuse. The first step in solving any complex problem is to identify its many parts, avoiding simple explanations and simple answers.

The ways we look at problems either help or hinder us. When we blame the drug problem only on youth, only on parents, only on criminals or only on society, we are looking for culprits and not for solutions. We lessen the chances that parents, children and society can work together to find solutions.

What can parents do? We can develop better ways of looking at the problem. We can develop more effective ways of communicating with our children. Sharing our new understanding, we help them develop their own. We can also take action to change some of the social conditions that lead to drug abuse. By demonstrating this broader approach in our thinking and in our actions, we are more likely to have an influence on the decisions our children make.

No booklet can tell you precisely how to talk to your child—what to say when. But we hope that the many examples included here of parent-child communication—examples of both effective and ineffective approaches—will enable you to see the challenge freshly and tackle it more perceptively.

Parents exert an influence on their children's behavior even when the children are not under parental surveillance. Though we will focus on drugs, the general guidelines to be discussed would, of course, apply in many other situations. In the pages to come we will suggest what approaches tend to work and which ones are likely to fail. In talking about drugs, we have to remember that we are always talking about a great deal more than drugs. We are talking about people and their relationships to each other, and we are conveying an attitude toward life in general.

DRUGS ARE NOT NEW

Drugs have been with us throughout recorded history. People in every era, in every generation and in every country have turned to drugs to reduce the pain of existence or to produce a special experience which was otherwise not available.

What is new in our time is the greater availability of drugs and their ever-increasing use by progressively younger age groups. In less than a decade, the use of drugs filtered down from isolated groups of adults to college students, to high school students and now to elementary school children. While drugs were once associated almost exclusively with poverty, drug use and drug addiction are now also found among the children of the well-to-do and the very rich. What was once an urban problem, largely confined to the East and West coasts of the United

States, has reached across the country to the smaller cities and rural areas.

IS IT AN "EPIDEMIC"?

The attention given to the drug problem in the mass media has fostered the belief that drug use has reached "epidemic" proportions. Many parents have concluded that nearly all young people are using drugs. This is not true. Drug abuse is not a "disease" that is "infectious" to all who are exposed to it. Young people are not equally vulnerable to drug use; some of them are not vulnerable at all.

Although larger numbers of young people are *trying* some drugs, a substantial number are not. Of those who try a drug such as marijuana one or more times, only a relatively small proportion proceed to use it regularly. Only a few of these go on to become very heavy users; even fewer "escalate" to harder drugs. The situation is roughly comparable to the use of alcohol, in which only a relatively small proportion of occasional drinkers move steadily in the direction of chronic alcoholism. This does not mean that the use of drugs by the young is inconsequential; it does mean adults have to be clear about the vast differences between drugs and the differences that exist between youngsters who try drugs once or twice and those who make them a way of life.

"DRUG CULTURE"
AND "YOUTH CULTURE"

The provocative terminology rampant today often interferes with clear thinking. "Drug culture" is one of those terms—a term that somehow moved from a convenient *description* of how drug users live to an explanation of drug use. The popular acceptance of a misleading concept like "drug culture" unwittingly dignifies the misuse of drugs. For some youngsters, it has tipped the scales in favor of drug use; they turn to drugs as a means of achieving identity through instant membership in this "new culture." This is one of the ways in which the reporting of a trend can actually contribute to its acceleration.

"Youth culture" is another term that obscures the issues. Most young people are not living in a totally isolated "youth culture," but many have adopted a distinctive life style. All young people have activities and experiences that are different from those of their parents. What magnifies the difference is that the young are more *visible* since the percentage of our population under twenty-five has increased enormously. Also, instant communication makes us constantly aware of their new ways of living. But the culture they are living in is the same culture we are all living in. They often react to it differently; in some cases, they react more perceptively. Yet, fundamentally, they are different from previous generations only to the extent that the times are different.

THE "GENERATION GAP"

The current emphasis on a "generation gap" has also tended to distort the relationship between parents and children. Some parents, apprehensive about the inexorable "gap" that they have been led to believe exists between them and their children, have become disheartened about the possibility of any genuine communication. Whenever understanding falters—as it occasionally must, even in the closest families—youngsters also are inclined to invoke the "generation gap."

We are now beginning to question whether that gap is nearly as wide as it is purported to be. There is considerable evidence that young people still are more like their parents than unlike them. Some "gap" between the generations is, and has always been, the inevitable result of the twenty or more years that separate one generation from another in time and in experience. Youth will always challenge the relevance of their elders' thinking about contemporary problems. Adults will always have the task of demonstrating that their thinking is indeed relevant.

UNSTEREOTYPING YOUTH

Our stereotyping of young people often interferes with our ability to talk with them meaningfully about drugs and to relate to them as individuals. Any preconceived idea of what a person is going to say and do may make communication with that person difficult or impossible. We don't really listen when we think we already know what we are going to hear. As a result, what we say to our children is likely to be as stereotyped—and as far off the mark—as our perception of them and their problems. One fifteen-year-old boy puts it this way:

> My parents have this idea that if you let your hair grow and wear jeans, you're part of the drug scene. All they seem to notice about me these days is how I look. I don't think they believe me when I say that me and my best friend have never tried pot, not even once. Funny, one of the squarest looking guys in our class is a pusher. I guess they wouldn't believe that, either, if I told them.

We cannot hope to understand the younger generation unless we stop stereotyping them. If we yield to the temptation to bunch youngsters into easy categories, we blind ourselves to the nuances of behavior that reveal to us what an individual young person is really thinking and feeling. We also invite hostility from the young.

Nothing could be further from the truth than the assumption that all young people are very much alike. Young people are as different from each other as their elders are—in temperament, personality, character and motivation. What they have in common is exposure to a large number of stresses that make growing into adulthood a hazardous journey.

SPECIAL STRESSES ON YOUTH

Young people today live under different and greater stresses than recent generations. Our generation was faced with a war, but it was one to which we could more easily make a commitment. Our generation was faced with the necessity of acquiring an education under conditions that were sometimes difficult and frustrating; but the relevance of education at every level was never so seriously questioned. Our generation had its doubts about where the world was going; but the doubts were not so fundamental and pervasive.

Every generation has had to face uncertainties about the future. For this younger generation, however, the areas of uncertainty have multiplied. They have grown up under the threat of nuclear destruction and the threat of a military draft law. Also, they are a generation of surplus people in the sense that we do not need their labor. They have too few opportunities for the kind of work, paid or volunteer, that makes true independence possible.

THE NEED FOR
A NEW "DRUG ETHIC"

Young people today live in a time of rapidly advancing technology, one small part of which is the development and availability of drugs. We now have at our disposal a stunning array of pills and potions to induce sleep or wakefulness, to allay depression, boredom, apathy, anxiety, tension and irritability, and to cure disease. An essential problem with drugs is the problem we face with many of our scientific achievements: how do we use them wisely?

Although we have made impressive advances in the technology of drugs, we have not made comparable advances in arriving at an acceptable code of ethics regarding their use. In fact, we are living in a culture that has made the indiscriminate use of drugs a respectable "solution" to a wide variety of human problems. Advertisements, especially television commercials, constantly parade this idea before our youth.

It is alarming—but not altogether surprising—that a number of young people have turned to drugs to cope with the traditional stresses of adolescence that have been magnified by contemporary life. Drugs have historically provided chemical solutions whenever we have despaired of other means of solving our human problems. The young now use different drugs from those that former generations used. And they seek, through drugs, somewhat different experiences. But the sanction for using drugs as a means to escape life's harsher aspects was established long before they were born. In all honesty, we cannot say that the young have created the drug problem. They have inherited it.

The drug problem is more dramatically visible in the young, but not confined to them. Drug misuse today is only one symptom of a widespread discontent with our society that afflicts people of all ages, classes and colors. The drug problem is not a problem for which parents, or their children, alone, can be held responsible; it needs to be viewed, and dealt with by all responsible members of society as part of the general malaise of our time.

COMMUNICATION THAT WORKS

Very little can be accomplished by belaboring our youngsters with prohibitions and warnings. They need information, calmly offered, about the real dangers—including the legal hazards—involved in using any of the various drugs to which they might have access.

Even quite young children tend to see through "scare" tactics. Exaggeration is always found out sooner or later and usually results in some breakdown of trust and communication.

What is urgently needed is open, honest and continuing communication between parents and children about all the things that matter to them. In a home where such verbal give and take abounds, there will be many opportunities for children and their elders to talk thoughtfully, and with mutual respect, about the social as well as the individual problems that drive some youngsters to drugs.

Why
Youngsters
Misuse Drugs

2

Listening carefully to young people has always been the first step in determining how to guide them. What the young themselves say about drugs gives us valuable clues to how we can best help our children avoid misusing them.

In youngster's first-hand accounts of their experiences with drugs, we usually see a chain of events, shaped by many factors in the child's personality, his family and his social environment, which gradually moves him toward drugs or away from them. It is important that we understand how many variables can affect this process. For example, some youngsters who seem to be emotionally unstable and hence, presumably, more susceptible to drugs may never have a problem with them, perhaps only because they are lucky enough not to be subjected to extreme pressures to use drugs in their particular community or peer group. Other youngsters, not at all the most rebellious or disturbed, can be thrown into a climate of drug use at a difficult period in their lives. These combined pressures will be too great for them to resist. Individual ability to withstand pressure varies, of course, but under sufficient stress almost everyone can be said to be drug-prone.

Another reality is frequently overlooked: young people *decide* to use drugs because this seems to be the best choice available to them. True, some young children are introduced to drugs by irresponsible older children or adults at an age when they really do not know what they are doing. But for most youngsters, there is a moment when a decision is made. Often made under stress, often made with inadequate information, it is nevertheless a decision. Only when the young person uses drugs to the point where psychological dependency or physical addiction develops is his power to decide weakened.

Bad decisions as well as "bad influences" are at the core of the drug problem. As parents, we have to be sensitive to all the potentially harmful influences our youngsters may be exposed to, but we cannot afford to blame the drug problem on environmental forces only. Young people are not simply passive victims of the influence of others; nor do they simply mirror social or family problems. They must be helped to see that they are actively responsible for making the decisions that determine the course of their lives.

A MATTER OF DEGREE

Once a youngster has tried drugs, he is not "doomed." Changing events and his own changing needs can move him to make a different choice, this time in the service of his healthier self. Sometimes this seems to happen out of the blue. More often, it requires the intervention of parents or of others who care about the youngster and sense that he is troubled. In a very real sense, one of the causes of the drug problem—and other problems—is nonintervention or the wrong kind of intervention during a critical period in a child's life.

If we look at drug misuse as a *process*—a chain of events that takes a while to happen—we begin to realize how many opportunities we have to step in and change the direction in which our children are moving. We cannot make our children's decisions for them, but we can become better at discerning when and how to act in order to influence their decisions. In the following first-person accounts of youngsters' experience with drugs, you will notice examples of opportunities well used—and of opportunities missed—by parents and others.

PRESSURE FROM PEERS

Almost every young person has a need to be accepted by others of his age. The experience of moving from "belonging" in the family to "belonging" in the wider world of one's peers is critically important to personal and social development. Every generation of young people has gone about fulfilling this task in its own way. Some young people, however, seem to have a greater need for the reassurance—or sense of "identity"—that acceptance by their peers provides.

In every community, there is usually at least one boy or girl who has tried the forbidden and is ready to encourage others to do the same. Sometimes it's cheating or stealing; sometimes it's sex; sometimes it's drugs.

For a number of youngsters, one of the most pressing reasons for experimenting with drugs is a need to belong to a group who are already taking drugs. This may be coupled with unusually strong curiosity, or ignorance about the effects of drugs, or with a need to take risks. This fifteen-year-old girl, who lives in a small town in California, was edged toward drugs by wanting to be in with the group:

> I had two close friends and they started hanging around with a group of kids at school who were smoking pot. I talked to them about it, but they said I was jealous because they were moving out on me and joining a group I was too straight for. I need friends, too. If you don't have the same interests, you're out. You have to show them you're not a square.

Sometimes the pressure comes not from a group but from a special friend. Girls who have been led to believe that having and keeping a boyfriend is an urgent social necessity, may be especially vulnerable. They will use drugs—or at least try them—in order to hold onto a relationship that provides status. This fourteen-year-old Los Angeles girl seemed to think she had no alternatives:

> I smoked pot with my boyfriend and then he wanted to try LSD. I was scared but he told me that if I didn't go along with him, he'd find a girl who would. Other kids told me there wasn't anything to worry about— that you just see lots of colors and different shapes, like the posters you see around.

In Gary, Indiana, another fourteen-year-old rationalizes her decision to try drugs with her boyfriend by attempting to reassure herself that drugs are not dangerous:

> I had a boyfriend who was on drugs. He was in a hospital for it but didn't stop. He was

after me to try drugs and I thought that he seemed all right, so it couldn't be true that drugs harm you. In fact, they helped him to feel more confident when his grades went down at school.

DRUG EDUCATION
AS A COUNTERFORCE

Young people are more apt to resist being pressured by their friends into experimenting with drugs if they have been adequately educated about them. In contrast to youngsters who go along with the crowd in drug experimentation, one thirteen-year-old Ohio boy says:

Things were getting to a point in my school where everybody was interested in drugs and daring everybody to try them. Then we had this course in drug abuse. I sure think it helped a lot of us. It gave us real facts which are very different from what you hear around. They didn't lie to us by saying pot is just as dangerous as LSD. When somebody really tells you straight, you don't have to experiment.

Other youngsters get their drug education at home. This fourteen-year-old boy from a Massachusetts town also displays resources that come from close family ties:

I was going with a group of kids who started on grass and then moved to other drugs. I didn't want any part of it so they started calling me names like *I* was some sort of freak. I'm lucky because I can talk to my parents about anything. I want friends who think I'm great but for the right reasons. I can also stand being alone—without friends—for a while.

What emerges in the experiences of many young people who are under pressure to experiment with drugs is that accurate information—but not exaggeration—about the potential dangers of drugs can often counteract the temptation to try them. But the child has to trust his sources of information. The capacity to trust *any* source has been impaired in this thirteen-year-old girl who lives in a small town in Kentucky:

> What's so bad about drugs all of a sudden? Most parents take drugs. They're supposed to help you, give you energy, get you through a bad day, things like that. You stop listening to people when they tell you to do one thing and you see them doing another.

MODELS FOR DRUG USE

Again, no single factor can be isolated as the major reason for drug use among the young. But, one thing that seems to encourage some youngsters to experiment with drugs is that drug taking is routine in their families. A fifteen-year-old boy from Bridgeport, Connecticut, reports:

> In my house, you can't sneeze without getting a pill. My mother is always taking something for headaches and my father is always taking something to keep awake to get his work done at night. They're not drunks but they sure drink a lot. So, now I'm a criminal for smoking pot?

Many youngsters are keenly aware of the inconsistencies in our thinking about drugs. In the words of a fifteen-year-old girl, who lives in Corpus Christi, Texas:

If you want to be scared out of your skull, take a look at what alcohol does to the liver. Diet pills, coffee and cigarettes, even aspirin, aren't good for you either, but you don't see parents going into a frenzy about these things.

In an upstate New York town, a fifteen-year-old boy sees the irony of his mother's response to the "discovery" that he has been smoking marijuana:

I never took anything, but I said I did to some other kids—just to be smart, I guess. This girl I was going with thought it was the truth and began writing me letters about how I was wrecking my life and I should stop. Then my mother found them and really freaked out. I couldn't get through to her. She's still taking tranquilizers from the shock. Wow!

A tacit endorsement of drug use may come, unwittingly, not only from parents but also from celebrities whom the young idolize, from magazines and newspapers which sensationalize the drug problem, and from TV commercials. An astute thirteen-year-old boy from Atlanta, Georgia, comments:

We're not supposed to take drugs but TV is full of commercials showing people running for a pill because something is bugging them. All the magazines write it up [the drug problem] as if to warn you, but they go on about some rock star dying of an overdose of drugs and make it sound like something real groovy. It's not teenagers who are crazy. It's people.

MODELS FOR RESPONSIBILITY

Not all youngsters who detect inconsistencies between what our society says and does about drug use are tempted to experiment injudiciously. A seventeen-year-old says:

> Sure, there's a lot of hypocrisy about drugs today. Every age has its hang-ups. Look at the Victorians. My parents aren't hypocrites, like some I know. They like their cocktails before dinner, even though they admit alcohol is a drug, but they know their limits. My dad takes antihistamines regularly during the hay fever season. Those little pills keep him from being a semi-invalid. The way I've grown up, I've learned what drugs can do *for* you as well as *to* you. I don't think I'll ever go off the deep end with drugs. I think I'll be pretty much like my parents that way.

Another youngster, fourteen, indicates that her close relationship with her parents is continuing to affect her conduct in general, even though she is moving away from her parents in some areas:

> I don't agree with my parents in everything. I'm not religious like they are. When I told them a while back I wasn't going to be confirmed, they were very disappointed. But they understand I'm still me, their daughter. They brought me up to think and behave responsibly and I'm trying—like I'm not into drugs, or anything like that.

ESCAPE FROM TENSION
OR BOREDOM

A number of youngsters use drugs for the same reasons that adults use them: they are bored and want a boost; they are tense or jittery and want something to calm them down. A few seem to be in a state of chronic, low-grade depression and turn to drugs to make them "happy." This is the way a fifteen-year-old girl from Ann Arbor, Michigan, puts it:

> I've tried pot, hash and goofballs. They're very relaxing and a beautiful experience. How else can you get something like this?

Another girl—a sixteen-year-old who lives in Pennsylvania—has experimented with other kinds of drugs and expresses similar feelings:

> I started on pot and then one day when I was feeling down, a friend handed me a couple of bennies [amphetamines] and said they would give me a high. They sure did. Then I found LSD was my bag. Where else can you get that beautiful feeling that you get on drugs, as if you could fly into all those colors around you? Where?

In describing their attraction to drug use, these young people convey their need for a "beautiful" experience. Also, significantly, they seem to be asking for alternatives to drugs: "How else can you get something like this?" "Where?" Parents have to hear these questions as real—genuine pleas for help in finding other rewarding experiences—not simply expressions of defiance.

REBELLION AGAINST PARENTS

A few youngsters, over the years, build up intense automatic resistance to parental authority—and authority in general. They feel compelled to do whatever is forbidden as a means of asserting their independence. They are usually youngsters who have not been given enough opportunities to test their wings appropriately; the limits set on their behavior have been too rigid, too strict or too capricious.

Other youngsters take drugs because they want to get a rise out of their parents. Drug use becomes a form of aggression, a way of getting attention, as this fifteen-year-old New York City girl clearly reveals:

> I've been on drugs for three years—since I was twelve. Why do I do it? I don't know. My parents found out and sent me to a shrink. That's supposed to mean they care—I guess they do. I just wish they would show it so I could feel it. My parents think I'm rebelling against something, but they don't know what. It's them. Not that they're strict. It's just that they're not really there and you feel you have to jump up and down and scream before they really notice.

Such "rebellious" youngsters are really rebelling not against parental authority but against what they experience as parental indifference.

DESPAIR

Some youngsters express very clearly their need to escape pressures that they find unendurable. In recalling his early attraction to drugs, a seventeen-year-old boy from a small town in Connecticut observes:

> A lot of grownups say that teenagers don't know what they're doing and are only looking for "kicks." What does that mean? I know why I decided to take drugs. I couldn't stand the rat race in school and

looking forward to more of the same. Doesn't everyone need to feel happy and peaceful some of the time? I was going out of my head feeling angry and no place to go. With the help of my doctor and my family I'm trying to do it another way but I don't know. I'm not sure I can make it. There's too much.

MULTIPLE CAUSES

The factors contributing to drug misuse are complex and varied. Youngsters who use drugs habitually almost always have more than one reason for doing so. They differ from each other in their reasons for using drugs, in the drugs they choose and in their physiological and psychological reactions to them.

Not one, but many forces operate to determine which way an individual will go at any given time in his development. This complexity is what makes traditional research studies so limited in the answers they can provide through even the most detailed statistical analysis.

Research studies do not show that a particular personality type is associated with drug misuse. One observation that is made rather consistently is that those who are drawn to drugs are immature. With regard to youngsters, this may be true, but it is not a very useful insight. It merely maintains that young people misuse drugs because they are young. The real question remains: why in our time are young people more vulnerable?

We do not see any pattern of causes either in the social environment or in the families of youngsters who use drugs excessively. This could mean that the drug problem is so complex that it resists ordinary analysis. Or it may mean that we have to look at the problem from a different point of view.

REDEFINING DEPRIVATION

When drug abuse and drug addiction were associated with poverty, it was easy to link drugs with deprivation. Now that many of the youngsters who turn to drugs come from affluent families that "have given them everything," the idea of deprivation seems absurd. Yet, we may have to take a second look at what we mean by deprivation and consider that many of our young people who "have everything" may indeed be missing much of what is necessary to healthy growth and development.

In the reasons they give for drug abuse, youngsters are expressing the absence of something they need to give their lives meaning and purpose. Those who take drugs because they are "bored" are really saying that they are depressed and apathetic because they lack activities that interest and engage them. Those who say they need drugs to reduce tension are telling us that their problems are overwhelming and that they know of no other way to handle them. When drugs are needed to feel "high," it suggests that there are too few opportunities to feel exhilarated by life without drugs.

Whatever their reasons for using drugs, all youngsters express—in one way or another—their need for guidance from their parents and from other adults. They have questions about drugs and about themselves and questions about the world in which they live. These questions must be answered in cooperation with adults who respect young people's concerns, have a perspective on the problem and a knowledge of drugs.

A
Discriminating
Look At Drugs
3

One difficulty parents face in trying to achieve a rational perspective on drugs is that *all* drugs commonly abused by young people are often lumped together as if they had the same effects, were used for the same reasons and posed the same dangers. As a result, the word "drug" sometimes triggers off in a worried parent a variety of reactions that may be inappropriate to the situation at hand.

We cannot afford to disqualify ourselves, through lack of information, from acting effectively to protect our young against the dangers of drug abuse. We have to look discriminatingly at drugs and see what distinguishes one from the other, both in terms of their effects and the reasons they appeal to youngsters. With this knowledge, we are in a better position to communicate with our children.

Sniffing Inhalants:
The "Drugs" of the Very Young

Youngsters are notably swayed by fads. In a society in which there is so much talk of "getting high," it is not surprising that even the very young are tempted to experiment. The fads in inhalants keep changing; they have included sniffing glue, gasoline, paint thinner, cleaning fluid, nail polish remover, hair spray and furniture polish—substances that are easy to come by in many households.

THE EFFECTS

A few whiffs of glue or gasoline may produce a pleasant sensation and giggly, cheerful, excited behavior which is comparable to mild intoxication. But the body builds tolerance to these inhalants, just as it does to the so-called "hard" drugs. Increasing amounts are needed to produce the same effect.

With excessive or prolonged use, inhalants can cause serious damage to a youngster's liver or kidneys. By freezing the larynx and the respiratory system, the gas in spray products can kill in seconds. The number of deaths from inhalants is not large; this does not negate the need for strong preventive measures at school and at home.

WHAT CAN PARENTS DO?

Children who use inhalants are likely to be in the younger age groups—some as young as six and seven. They are motivated by curiosity and pressure from their peers to try something new "for kicks." Many of them are unaware of the dangers. Early education about this hazard, combined with sensible parental supervision, is important.

As with all drug education, the best approach to sniffing is a calm, matter-of-fact one. It cannot be repeated too often how careful we should be to avoid exaggeration and "scare" tactics. If our children hear us exaggerating dangers, we lose credibility with them.

It's usually sufficient to tell your child before he starts school that sniffing is one of many dangerous situations to which he will be exposed in the course of growing up. Just as he must learn to be careful crossing the street and handling tools, so he must learn to avoid dangerous drugs as part of becoming responsible and more grown-up. If your child is curious about why sniffing is dangerous, you can explain the potential dangers described above. You might want to put this within the context of the pains *you* take to avoid inhaling the fumes of hair spray, cleaning fluid, paint thinner or some other substance that is useful but can be harmful when mishandled.

When adequate facts are provided by parents, most children will avoid, or stop, sniffing. A small number will continue to use inhalants even after they have been told of the dangers. These youngsters are acting, not out of ignorance, but from a desire to harm themselves. They require not only more careful supervision but, usually, psychological treatment to get at the causes of a compulsion to do what is forbidden and dangerous.[1]

Marijuana: Fact and Fiction

Popular thinking about marijuana reveals some stereotypes that tend to separate the generations. To a number of young people, marijuana has come to represent a great deal more than an intoxicant that may or may not be harmful. It has become a cause, a rallying point for rebellion and a badge of freedom. For a number of adults, the attack on marijuana is really an attack on youth itself—on a new life style that is perplexing and disturbing. We must move beyond this polarized thinking if we are to develop a productive approach to the problem. It further complicates matters that a great deal of misinformation about marijuana is bandied about on both sides.

THE EFFECTS

Marijuana—also known as "pot," "grass," "tea" and "dope"—is a product of the common hemp plant, *cannabis sativa.* It is related to, but considerably less potent than hashish, or "hash," which is derived from the same plant. Marijuana acts as a mild intoxicant or as an hallucinogen, depending upon the amount that is used and upon the predisposition of the user. Some individuals are sensitive to minute quantities, whereas others can take relatively large doses without apparent effect. The user's personality,

[1] Sources for obtaining psychological or medical help are suggested on page 71.

his emotional state, his expectations, the setting in which he takes the drug and his previous experience with it blend to affect his reactions. This complexity makes it difficult to predict the drug's effects.

In ordinary low doses, marijuana usually produces a mild euphoria. At the start of a "high," many marijuana smokers are giggly, even hilarious; later they become more passive and may lapse into quiet reverie. Most marijuana users report alterations in sense perception. They say they see colors and shapes more vividly; they report hearing subtleties in music not usually apparent to them; time seems to stand still. These experiences are characteristic of the majority of low-dosage marijuana users. Some of these, however, who are emotionally or biochemically fragile, have unpredictably severe reactions. Temporary panic and even hallucination can occur.

Although the effects we *do* know about seem harmless enough, we lack sufficient evidence from research concerning the long-range physical and psychological effects of marijuana use. Conclusions about the effects of different strengths of marijuana can be reached only when we have more evidence. Research designed to give us this information is underway.

WHO USES IT?

It has been estimated that more than six million young people of college and high school age in the United States have tried marijuana at least once. Obviously, all of these youngsters are not emotionally disturbed. A teenager picked up in a marijuana raid may be a "good" student or a "bad" one; he may come from a "good" home or a "troubled" one; he may be emotionally stable or unstable. Smoking pot has become so widespread and prestigious among the young that the temptation to experiment is very strong, often irresistible. Parents should anticipate that well-balanced, reasonably mature youngsters may try marijuana.

Most marijuana smokers use it occasionally and continue to function in school and at work. They find it easy to obtain through friends or other young people. They use marijuana as a means of relaxing, to be used with discrimination, comparable to their parents' drinking a martini before dinner. On the other hand, some are heavy users who organize their lives and their friendships around marijuana. It becomes an unhealthy preoccupation, and other interests and activities dwindle. In these instances, excessive marijuana use is symptomatic of other adolescent difficulties. Attention has to be paid to the sources of all of a youngster's problems rather than to one symptom alone. This may require professional help.

LEGAL STATUS

Under our laws there are still severe criminal penalties for the use or possession of marijuana. Marijuana was outlawed by the Marijuana Tax Act of 1937, a law which is still in effect. This act was passed as a consequence of lurid, misleading testimony from narcotics agents linking the drug to violence, crime and insanity. Despite the fact that few judges impose maximum sentences, lengthy jail terms have been known to be given to youthful first offenders. These punitive measures, disproportionate to the known dangers of the drug, still continue. The young sometimes seem oblivious to the fact that smoking pot can saddle them with a police record, a serious matter in itself, even if they manage to avoid going to jail.

WHAT CAN PARENTS DO?

Crisis situations can be productive. They can provoke parents and children into communicating more honestly with each other than either had hitherto considered possible. Talking openly about disturbing, emotionally-laden issues often moves families to new levels of intimacy. A sixteen-year-old boy says:

> After my parents got me released in their custody [from jail, on a drug-possession charge], they went into their usual what-have-we-done-to-deserve-this act and I told them to cut the shit. I must have been pretty desperate. Things were sort of tense for a while. I let it all hang out and they did too. When we got home we were talking to each other like we haven't done in years. Would you believe my parents actually have a sense of humor and all of a sudden I can make them laugh?

What can parents do? We can talk with—not at—our children. We can listen to them, and we can show by our attitude that we want them to speak frankly, especially when we don't happen to share their views. It is up to us, the older more experienced generation, to create and maintain an atmosphere in our home that insures continuing, open, honest discussion. This is the only way we can hope to know what our children are thinking and what is going on in their lives.

Parents who do not trust their children to tell them what they are doing, often resort to "snooping." They listen in on telephone calls, steam open mail and search through drawers. These parents lose sight of the fact that information gathered in this way cannot be used productively. One has to create a climate of trust for dialogue, and a parent eliminates the possibility of such a climate if he has acted in a way that demonstrates mistrust.

There are two common misconceptions about what makes for good relationships between parents and young people. At one extreme is the "pal" concept, which is epitomized by the parent who smokes pot with his child in order to demonstrate that he is not an old fogey. We lose standing with our children when we try to act *their* age and also flout the law. At the other extreme is the "authoritarian" parent, who feels he can exercise his parental responsibility only by pronouncing inflexible judgements based on his superior age and knowledge. This approach fosters resentment and rebellion.

Good human relations are characterized by mutual respect and an acknowledgement of different levels of knowledge, experience and competence. To insure real communication between parents and children we must show in our actions our belief that our children have the capacity to think and reason clearly. We must also demonstrate our own ability to think and reason clearly, which means to concentrate on important issues and let some things slide.

PARENTAL FEARS

Many parents are unnecessarily anxious because they fear that marijuana is addictive, that it is physically harmful and that it inevitably leads to the use of stronger drugs. The evidence is that marijuana does not produce physical dependency and is, therefore, nonaddictive. Research on the physical effects of prolonged usage, now in its early stages, has not yet produced significant evidence of physical harm— though it also has not eliminated this possibility.

The belief that marijuana usually leads to the use of more dangeous drugs is a consequence of anxiety about the *possibility* of such a process. It is also a misinterpretation of the fact that many heroin addicts have smoked marijuana somewhere along the way to heroin. Many heroin addicts are also known to have been heavy users of alcohol, but this does not warrant the conclusion that alcohol or marijuana inevitably sets the user on a course towards addiction to "hard" drugs.

REAL RISKS

Many young people are inclined to minimize some of the potential physical, emotional and legal hazards of marijuana. They may discount the dangers of driving under the influence of marijuana. To date, there are no reliable statistics concerning the relationship between marijuana intoxication and auto accidents, but any drug that alters a driver's perception of time and distance is clearly a driving hazard. Young people may dismiss lightly the possibility of inadvertently acquiring marijuana that has been adulterated. This does happen. Any drug that must be obtained illegally—even though the immediate source may be a friend—poses the hazard that it might be contaminated.

Young people may also be aware of the extent to which habitual marijuana use can limit their psychological development. When marijuana is used as an easy way out of anxiety, restlessness, self-questioning—troubles traditionally associated with adolescence—normal adolescent development may be slowed down or postponed indefinitely. The task of growing up cannot be accomplished without a certain amount of struggle and pain. It is by fighting through his problems as they occur that an adolescent learns who he is and builds strengths to cope with the inevitable stresses of later life. Although a young person may argue that drugs are "where it's at," their use can make it impossible for the user to know truly where *he's* at in his emotional development. What may be circumvented is the necessary process of keeping in touch with oneself and one's feelings.

SHOULD THE LAWS AGAINST MARIJUANA BE REPEALED?

There is enormous controversy as to whether or not the laws against marijuana should be repealed. Those who favor repeal argue that the present laws are excessively severe and unenforceable and—like the prohibition of alcohol in the past—encourage crime and disrespect for the law. Many responsible citizens favor legalization, with the same kinds of controls that operate in the distribution and sale of alcohol. Opponents are reluctant to add one more legal intoxicant to to those already used and abused in our society. They want to wait for further evidence.

Arguments as to the justice of the laws and their penalties must not obscure the fact that marijuana is still illegal. Parents have the responsibility of informing and reminding children of this reality and all that it may entail.

LSD: Mind-Altering Drug

LSD is perceived by many young people as a glamor drug, and it has become difficult to separate the facts from the romantic fiction surrounding its use. Many youngsters are convinced that they know all the real facts. Parents have the task of being thoroughly informed.

WHAT IT IS

LSD (also known as "acid," "sunshine" or "white lightning") is a colorless, odorless and tasteless chemical. It comes in liquid or powdered form or in capsules of various colors. Usually dissolved in fruit drinks or added to food such as sugar cubes or cookies, pure LSD is so potent that a tiny drop constitutes a sufficient dose for several users.

THE EFFECTS

LSD produces hallucinatory effects—sensory experiences that are not caused by external stimuli. A variety of other substances also produce similar mind-altering effects; the two most widely-known are *mescaline*, which comes from the peyote cactus, and *psilosybin,* which comes from the Mexican "sacred mushroom."

LSD "trips" start within a half-hour or more after taking the drug and last for varying periods of time. The effects differ from one individual to another, depending upon the dosage and upon the user's personality, his expectations and the conditions surrounding his use of the drug. Sometimes LSD is taken in isolation; more often several people share the experience, making a group ritual of it.

No one is certain how LSD acts upon the nervous system. Sensory impressions seem to flood the brain, unrestrained by the usual sorting-out or braking mechanisms. Some LSD users report unusual, pleasant, even ecstatic experiences; colors explode, objects bend and flow, music can be "seen" as well as heard. On the other hand, very bad experiences are frequent, and medical intervention is often necessary.

Even reasonably well-balanced adults can have nightmarish experiences under LSD. These may include terrifying sensations that their bodies are dissolving and feelings that they are going insane. Although LSD is touted as a "love drug," some people become extremely hostile and suspicious under its influence.

Another bizarre feature of this drug is that, without additional doses, an LSD experience may recur spontaneously several days or months later. These "flashbacks" may be triggered by bright lights or music or emotional stress. They usually last for a few moments only, but the effects can be terrifying.

As far as anyone knows, LSD is not addictive. Some studies have indicated a likelihood of long-lasting damage to chromosomes. But more research is needed before we can reach any definite conclusions. Permanent chromosome damage from LSD use is at present a possibility although not an established scientific fact.

Any drug that is so unpredictable in its effects is unsafe. Unstable people of any age may react to the LSD experience with severe and lasting anxiety or depression. They sometimes have to be confined in a mental institution for months, or years. Because LSD alters perception and judgment, its users sometimes have accidents resulting in serious injury, even death. The risks are greater for young people who are immature and unstable—that is, the very young people who may be most drawn to an experience that promises quick self-realization or "instant religion."

SOME IMPORTANT ISSUES

Those who use LSD often believe they are engaged in a search for enlightenment. They see it as a means of transcending the material world and finding new meanings in life. This quest for a spiritual or mystical experience, reflected in the revival of interest in Eastern mysticism, is an interesting contemporary phenomenon. It represents a reaction against the materialistic values of our society.

Some LSD users say they are challenging a value system that gives top priority to the possession of material goods and social prestige. They argue further that the kinds of aggression and competitiveness encouraged by our values have made us incapable of cooperating with or loving each other. They believe that LSD holds the promise of opening us up to new ways of relating to each other and a richer inner life.

It would be a mistake to disparage the positive motives behind this quest. But it would be equally irresponsible to fail to question the use of LSD as a means of genuinely resolving personal and social problems. The dangers of LSD are real. As young people are becoming increasingly aware of these dangers, its popularity has markedly diminished.

"Up" and "Down" Drugs: Mood Manipulation

Every time you look at the boob-tube there's some lady taking a pill because her kids are skating all over the kitchen linoleum. There are other pills you take when the relatives come over—pills to calm you down, pills to pep you up.

This observation from a thirteen-year-old reflects the sanction for mood manipulation to which the present generation has been exposed. The models for solving problems through drug use come not only from parents and peers but also from advertising.

Tons of pep pills, diet pills, sleeping pills and tranquilizers are legally manufactured every year in the United States. When youngsters wish to experiment with the pills they call "ups" and "downs," they frequently have to go no further than the family medicine chest. Youngsters in some communities arrive at "potluck" pill parties with a sizeable contribution from their parents' supplies.

Stimulants and sedatives have their legitimate medical uses, but it is generally agreed that these drugs are being over-prescribed and over-used by large numbers of people seeking to avoid the ordinary stresses of everyday life. Taken without medical supervision, these drugs can be extremely dangerous. They can cause physical and mental damage, even death. Unlike another extremely dangerous drug, heroin, they are legal, easily available and relatively inexpensive.

WHAT ARE THEY?

The "up" drugs are stimulants. They include amphetamines, cocaine, caffeine and nicotine. Cocaine is a powerful stimulant which differs from other "up" drugs in that it is not available by prescription and is obtained through criminal sources.

The most commonly used amphetamines are

Benzedrine ("bennies"), Dexedrine ("dexies"), Methedrine ("meth" or "speed" or "crystal"), and Dexamyl (which combines an amphetamine with a barbiturate). They are prescribed medically for relief of fatigue, for weight control, and as mood elevators for depressed or mentally ill people. Although it happens rather slowly, a large degree of tolerance can develop.

One of the most insidious dangers of the "up" drugs is that they mask the symptoms of fatigue, so that a user may push himself beyond his physical endurance, going without food or sleep for several days. When the effects of the drug subside, extreme exhaustion and depression commonly follow. Taking more pills to counteract these reactions sets up a cycle of drug use that is hard to break.

Chronic users of amphetamines characteristically lose weight and become progressively more tense and jittery, more irritable, suspicious and aggressive. They tend to be nonstop talkers. Weakened by days without food or sleep, they are easy prey to infections. Extremely heavy users may end up with a full-blown amphetamine psychosis—confused, frightened and out of touch with reality. Dangers of infection and overdose are increased when amphetamine is injected for a faster, more powerful "high."

The "down" drugs are depressants. They include barbiturates, tranquilizers and alcohol. Barbiturates, sometimes called "barbies" or "goofballs," include Seconal, Nembutal and phenobarbital. They often figure in suicide, intentional and unintentional. Tranquilizers are familiar to us under such trade names as Miltown, Equanil and Librium. Barbiturates and tranquilizers are prescribed to relieve tension and produce sleep. Excessive use can result in tolerance, physical dependency and addiction. Barbiturates are particularly dangerous when coupled with alcohol or other drugs; one drug boosts the action of the other, sometimes with fatal results.

WHAT CAN PARENTS DO?

The widespread use of these drugs for medically prescribed purposes tends to obscure the hazards involved in using them. A person who is dependent upon a drug for mood changes is likely to use other drugs to try to balance his precarious emotional and physical states. It is not uncommon for the habitual user of barbiturates to add amphetamines to his drug-taking regime. If he is too "down," he takes an "up" to correct the situation, sometimes adding alcohol in the hopeless effort to achieve a perfect blend of energy and freedom from tension. His own body becomes a laboratory in which he works like a mad scientist to find a panacea for all of his ills.

It is encouraging to note that many young people have become aware of the critical dangers of "up" and "down" drugs. "Speed Kills" is a warning issued to the young by the young. Amphetamines and barbiturates are not "glamor drugs" like LSD and the other hallucinogens; they do not share the aura of sophistication that continues to be attached to marijuana. In fact, "speed freaks" are the objects of some disdain by other young people.

If a young person continues to misuse these drugs habitually, after he has been given adequate information about their known dangers, it is most certainly a symptom of serious instability. The youngster is having developmental difficulties severe enough to warrant immediate and sustained psychological treatment.

All citizens should take steps to discourage advertisers from touting drugs as panaceas for all human problems. Parents need to be involved in these actions. Also, drug manufacturers should be pressed to account more responsibly for the distribution of "up" and "down" drugs. There is today a large black market in these pills.

Heroin: Escape to Oblivion

We used to believe that heroin addiction was a disease that grew out of the misery and hopelessness of poverty. But that explanation is insufficient now that a number of youngsters with material advantages have also turned to the drug. No parent can afford to be ignorant about what heroin is and what it does to its users.

WHAT HEROIN IS

Heroin is an opiate. (Users call it "scag," "smack," "junk," "horse," or "H.") It belongs to the family of pain-killing drugs derived from opium. It is powerfully addictive and becomes a consuming preoccupation in the lives of users.

Some medically useful pain-killing drugs, such as paregoric and codeine, are also derived from opium, but they are far less potent than heroin. There are also a number of man-made narcotics, like Demerol, that are similar to the opiates. They, too, are medically useful but much abused.

THE EFFECTS

Most young heroin addicts begin by sniffing or "snorting." In some neighborhoods, this starts as early as elementary school. Many of the youngsters lured into sniffing heroin think that it is not dangerous. Actually heroin passes quickly through the nasal membranes into the blood stream, and anyone with a special sensitivity to the drug can die from sniffing as easily as from injecting.

Heroin users may proceed next to "skin-popping," injecting heroin under the skin of fleshy parts of the arm or body. This is still not as drastic as injecting heroin into a vein; but as the user's body builds tolerance for the drug, his need for a more immediate effect nearly always causes him to progress to "mainlining."

Heroin injected into a vein gives an almost instantaneous sensation of pleasurable feeling. The "rush" lasts only about a minute and is succeeded by a period of drowsiness. The user may go "on the nod"—visibly nodding like someone who is half-asleep. For two or three hours, mental and physical activities are slowed down and the sharp edges of reality are blurred.

Not very long afterwards, the addict begins to worry about where his next "fix" is coming from, since his addiction often requires that he use the drug three or four times a day.

Heroin, except in special cases of sensitivity or overdose, does not seem to produce organic damage. The physical hazards, nevertheless, are formidable. Through shared needles, addicts spread hepatitis; they suffer from abscesses and collapsed veins; they sometimes die of tetanus. Because of their frantic search for the drug and their indifference to food, addicts frequently suffer from malnutrition and are unusually susceptible to pneumonia. Drugged so that they are less sensitive to pain, they may injure themselves and not know it. Deaths from overdose are reported daily. In New York City, heroin kills more young people than all the contagious diseases combined.

For the addict, getting and using heroin becomes a constant and time-consuming activity. The ordinary demands of school attendance or employment are usually too much for him to sustain. Addicts of school age often drop out or flunk out of school; it is the rare addict who holds onto a steady job. Legitimate work does not usually yield the forty or more dollars a day required for heroin, so the "junkie" frequently must resort to criminal activity. Heroin, itself, does not produce violent or criminal behavior, but its high cost and the enormous difficulties surrounding its use make criminal behavior its by-product.

WHERE DO YOUNGSTERS
GET HEROIN?

Heroin traffic is a complex and enormously profitable business. It is carried on through a loosely-organized network of practiced criminals, independent operators and local-level "junkie-pushers." By the time heroin reaches the user, it has changed hands many times, with sizeable jumps in profit along the way. Neighborhood pushers sell heroin in small transparent envelopes. These "bags" commonly cost five dollars, but smaller amounts at three and two dollars are widely available—reportedly to interest the younger trade. Most street dealers are themselves addicts and they push heroin to support their own drug habit. Pushers sell heroin more or less openly in many neighborhoods, and a network of sellers and buyers spreads from these areas to other parts of cities and towns—to schools, playgrounds, candy stores and other places where young people gather.

WHAT PARENTS CAN DO:
PREVENTION OF HEROIN ADDICTION

Curiosity, a love of danger, and a search for euphoria are only a few of the factors involved in heroin addiction. Youngsters who are ignorant of the consequences of experimenting with heroin may become habituated before they realize it can happen to them. Early and effective drug education is critical to the prevention of heroin addiction.

In their desire to protect their children, some parents avoid discussing heroin and other drugs altogether. Some even go so far as to discourage drug education in the schools. Heroin use is so widespread and so talked about that no child can be shielded from knowing about it; it is far better for him to get the facts correctly at home or at school.

Education is only one aspect of prevention. In addition, we have to take steps to reduce the stresses of life for some young people. The "typical" heroin addict is often said to be a person who is unable to stand life's ordinary stresses. For some young people today, the stresses are far from ordinary, and the horrendous difficulties of living in the drug world seem infinitely preferable to the real world. This can be true when that world is the ghetto, or when it is one furnished with comfortable material possessions but without purpose or meaning.

GETTING HELP
WITH A HEROIN PROBLEM

A young person who gets involved with heroin needs medical and psychological help. The kind of treatment he needs will depend on whether or not he is truly addicted and how well-motivated he is to stop taking the drug. Parents have to place themselves firmly and unshakeably on the side of the child's giving up the drug and entering treatment.

If you need counseling about heroin use, the best person to turn to first is probably your family doctor. Because of the growing concern about heroin within organized medical circles, family doctors are being given more information all the time to equip them to deal with this problem. Treatment centers are so overloaded that parents can almost never get the immediate help that they need for their child by going directly to such a center. They will often require some kind of stop-gap assistance until such time as more intensive treatment, if necessary, is available.

TREATMENT OF
HEROIN ADDICTION

Although the number of treatment facilities in the country is growing, there are still far too few. Currently there are two approaches to treating heroin addiction: total withdrawal from all drugs, or substitution of a more manageable drug. Both approaches require considerable and sustained psychological and social support from others.

A variety of voluntary treatment centers have been set up where addicts can live and work together to rid themselves permanently of their drug problems. In many of these treatment centers, such as Synanon, Daytop and Phoenix Houses, ex-addicts, themselves, provide leadership as well as proof that heroin addiction can be overcome. Some centers also have psychiatrists or other professionals in the program. Programs of this kind last from one to three years or more; there are always a number of dropouts. Because these programs are relatively new and often differ from each other in significant ways, it is not yet possible to assess the degree of success that various types of total withdrawal programs afford.

The drug-substitution method is aimed at enabling heroin addicts to function in their communities during treatment. The craving for heroin is satisfied by substituting methadone or other drugs. These substitute drugs are also physically addictive. They are, however, longer lasting in their effect, legally available and administered in a medical setting. Hence they may free the addict from his preoccupation with drug-getting and drug-taking and enable him to work or go to school. While the number of addicts in methadone programs is still relatively small, the percentage of those who continue in the program successfully is encouraging.

A MAJOR SOCIAL PROBLEM

No matter how effective we become in drug education and in treatment programs, we will still have to confront a crucial social problem that is reflected in all drug abuse. For some youngsters, the "drug scene" is better than the aimless boredom, emptiness and frustration of "real" life. Buying and pushing drugs, going through the rituals of using them and avoiding detection provide excitement and a kind of identity, even a test of courage and manhood. These youngsters need healthy opportunities to feel good and be somebody. With our help they have to change themselves, but we have to be responsible for making changes in the outside world as well.

Parental
Responsibility

4

Parenthood has always been difficult as well as rewarding. In the past several decades, medical progress has relieved us of many worries about our children's physical health and growth. Technology has made housekeeping less time-consuming and done away with some of the most tedious chores of child-rearing. These are no small blessings; but the same years that brought these changes also swept in a host of new problems.

Parents today rarely have the help of other adults in raising their children. The "extended family," with grandparents or aunts and uncles living under the same roof, or nearby, spread the responsibility for meeting the needs of children. Now, in the middle class, at least, such a family is almost nonexistent. This has reduced some kinds of family conflict but increased other tensions. Most families also lack the experience of having lifetime neighbors. Many children are no longer tied to communities where they are known and feel they belong. They often have to achieve their identity and their status through their ability to get along with other children. This means that they may feel a greater need to be accepted by their peers than earlier generations experienced.

At the same time that parents were being required to raise their children alone, they were being apprised of the many mistakes that they could make. Parenthood has become an extraordinary self-conscious occupation.

We used to think that problem children were born that way, and that behavior was entirely a matter of genes. Many parents found it a relief to view their children's difficulties in this light. As we moved on to understanding the role that environment also plays in shaping human behavior, we somehow came to focus more and more narrowly on parents as environment.

There is no question that parents exert a profound influence in the lives of their children. But ours is not the only influence; nor is it the most important influence at every stage in a child's development. When we consider what we can do to prevent our children from misusing drugs, we must remember that we are not solely responsible for all that happens to our youngsters and may not, alone, have the power to protect them from harm. We do have a responsibility, however, to interpret to them the other influences at work. In considering our responsibility for the current misuse of drugs, we must keep this perspective in mind.

WHEN DOES
DRUG EDUCATION BEGIN?

A child's education about drugs begins when he is a toddler and dangerous substances in the household—ammonia, insecticides, oven cleaner and the like, as well as the family's medicines—

are kept securely out of his reach. Like the early warnings that we give our children about knives, matches, hot stoves and boiling pots, warnings about the dangers of drugs are a routine part of the total education he gets from us to ensure his safety and survival. We relieve him of the bottle of aspirin that he manages to get hold of as quickly and firmly as we take away the paring knife that catches his fancy, and with much the same explanation: they are not playthings; they are dangerous if not used properly by persons old enough to know how.

As our children grow older, they learn that drugs are sometimes necessary; they go to a doctor or clinic and get shots to protect them from a variety of childhood diseases; they have sore throats and earaches and take a prescribed antibiotic to cure them. They also learn that drugs are not used for every ache and pain, but reserved for a time when they are really needed. In teaching our children to develop a discriminating view of drugs, it helps if we ourselves do not resort routinely to pills as a panacea for all our mild physical pains and psychic complaints.

PARENTS AS ROLE MODELS

Children take their cue from what we do as well as what we say. In our behavior, they see us either handling problems or evading them. The ways in which we characteristically meet the stresses of everyday life are central to their education about the use of drugs.

If we face up to challenges rather than avoid them and meet our responsibilities rather than evade them, our children are more likely to do the same. They assess us in terms of our whole approach to living and not just our pattern of drug use.

Being emotionally stable does not mean always being "cool, calm and collected." In fact, it requires the capacity to feel and express appropriately a wide range of feelings and moods that include irritability as well as good humor, sadness as well as happiness. Children are not damaged by exposure to this repertory of human feelings; they are enriched by it. They learn in the process that life entails frustration as well as satisfaction, sadness as well as joy. They learn to experience "highs" and "lows" as the normal ebb and flow of life.

IF OUR IMAGE IS "TARNISHED"

Parents are sometimes thrown by the charge that they are being hypocritical in their moralizing about youth and drugs. What about their own sleeping pills, diet pills, pep pills, tranquilizers, caffeine, nicotine and alcohol? Those who use drugs in moderation do not have to be apologetic, and they are in the best position to respond effectively.

Parents who depend heavily upon one or several drugs may be in for a harder time. They are likely to feel guilty and defensive and consequently are handicapped in discussing drugs with their children. It does not help in such cases to argue that alcohol, cigarettes and tranquilizers are not illegal. What is important is that our children understand that we do not approve of excessive use of drugs by any age group or any person, including ourselves. If we can concede this, we may be able to talk productively with our youngsters about the medical, social and psychological reasons why people become dependent upon drugs and what might be done about this. When we are honest with our children and admit our fallibility, they respect us. They are more apt to be influenced by what we say, not by what we have done.

In these painful confrontations with the young, we may find that in the course of helping them resolve their mixed feelings about using drugs, we are resolving some of our own. In any case, it would be what the young call a "cop-out" to avoid discussing drugs because of fears that by broaching the subject we will expose ourselves to uncomfortable questioning.

Even parents who have had or still have extremely serious problems with drugs are not necessarily disqualified from providing the guidance their children need. It makes the task more difficult but not impossible. Very few young people are interested in condemning their parents for past errors; they are much more interested in a candid discussion about drugs in which their parents demonstrate their ability to look objectively at their own drug use.

A fourteen-year-old says:

> I guessed a while back my mother was an alcoholic. She's been in and out of hospitals since I can remember. So when the two of them [parents] started warning me about drugs I let them have it. That's when

they told me my mother's problem is drugs, not alcohol. It really shook me at first. But now I admire her for being able to say it. At least we're talking more like a family these days.

TAKING A REASONABLE STAND

Some parents feel unqualified to give advice about the new drugs because they have had no direct experience with them. They may try drugs in an attempt to "understand" the experience, a gesture of good will that usually backfires. Most children want a greater show of strength than this. No matter how confident they appear, they are often uncertain about drug use and want parents who are willing to debate the issues—not middle-aged recruits to the drug scene.

It is absurd to contend that one needs direct experience with all drugs in order to take a valid position about them. There are a whole range of social problems—poverty, racial inequality, genocide—about which we have to take a stand although we may not have experienced them. If our children suggest that we're not qualified to talk about certain drugs because we've never tried them, we have an opportunity to drive home the difference between *knowing* through immediate experience and *knowledge,* which, among other things, makes it unnecessary for us to continually rediscover the laws of gravity or the effects of radiation.

Parents may differ about what constitutes a "reasonable stand" on some of the drugs available to the young today. Each of us has to talk with our children in our own way. It is our duty, however—not just our right—to tell our youngsters where we stand as well as why. Especially during the early adolescent years, this can be a very potent positive influence on the decisions they make. If we take our stands on various drugs individually rather than collectively, and we base these stands on reasons which we can convincingly document, our children are more likely to accept them.

PARENTAL ANXIETY

Young people are nonplused by the outbursts, the handwringing, even the hysterics, with which some parents greet the discovery that their child has been smoking marijuana. Instead of being drawn into a dialogue about the wisdom of drug use, such youngsters find themselves cast in the role of having to calm their parents and provide emotional support, much as if the adults were the children.

Parents have to acknowledge their anxiety but also become aware of the extent to which their anxiety may have grown out of proportion to the problem they face. The other extreme, of feeling or pretending no anxiety, is also fraught with difficulties. Over-anxious parents frequently bewilder their children; "cool" parents disappoint them. A good rule of thumb is to try to keep yourself under control, but proceed to express your concerns openly and frankly. This makes for the kind of authentic human encounter that most young people respond to with the best in themselves.

LEARNING TO LISTEN

We are accustomed to thinking of communication mainly in terms of what we say and how well we say it. Listening, on the other hand, is a communication skill that is relatively undeveloped in many people.

We need to work at listening to our children. This is especially true when the subject—like drugs—is emotionally charged. Anxiety often drives us to talk more and listen less at those very times when our youngsters are most in need of being heard. We also have to develop our capacity to listen for feelings as well as words. What seems like belligerence in a child is often uncertainty; what seems like an open-and-shut case of rejecting parental values is often a mask for a continuing need to be convinced. It is only when we really listen that our children develop confidence in our ability to help.

SUPPORTING STRENGTHS

In our understandable anxiety about the special strains on youth today, we can overlook some special strengths that young people have always had. Especially when they are young, human beings are resilient; they can bounce back, change direction, develop new attitudes, find new interests. They possess weaknesses but remarkable resoures as well. Parents and society aggravate weakness when it is their exclusive concern; strength is encouraged when it is looked for and given attention. Young people continue to give us evidence that their potential for health and growth is there to be tapped.

KNOWING OUR CHILDREN

It is not always easy for us to recognize when our children are under unusual stress and may therefore be more vulnerable to the temptation to try drugs. Occasionally, we see obvious pressures: approaching exams on which a great deal depends; uncertainties connected with starting to date; an upsurge of rivalry with a sibling. We can guess at other pressures: a close friend stops coming around and being mentioned, so we assume there has been a falling out. Such situations alert us to the need to be available, to be there but not intrude—ready to listen and support.

Sometimes there is no way for us to know that our youngster feels especially pressed, except as he shows this by seeming out of sorts. The fact that adolescents are often moody should not make us oblivious to their moods. Prying is justifiably resented. However, a genuinely meant, "Is something wrong?" or "Can I do something for you?" is unlikely to put a young person off. It can eventually, if not immediately, lead to his sharing his feelings with us.

KNOWING OURSELVES

Making an effort to know and understand youngsters is only one part of relating to them effectively. The other side of the equation is knowing ourselves. Parents are always better able to help their children when they are armed not only with facts and information but also with an awareness of their own feelings and attitudes. This is especially critical with regard to drugs because the subject has become so charged with emotion.

Young people who make drugs a way of life challenge some of our deepest assumptions about the way life should be lived. Our value system has been one that placed a high premium on ambition, hard work and achievement. To a number of adults, the use of drugs is a negation of all these values. Reinforcing this view, many young people who vehemently defend drugs also vehemently reject their parents' values. Even so, the conflict between these young people and their parents is often not as great as it appears. Many parents question the same values in our society that young people are questioning. They often differ in their views about the means by which worthwhile changes can be brought about.

If drugs are an escape for some youngsters, it makes sense to take a judicious look at what they are escaping from. Does the reality they are avoiding warrant an escape reaction? In some cases, we may concede that we cannot in good conscience ask them to "adjust to life"; the real need is to help them change reality so that it is more tolerable.

BASIC HUMAN VALUES

The drug question involves a number of very basic values. Youngsters want—and have the right to expect—that we will be conscientious and consistent in upholding our convictions about what is worthwhile in life. In the eyes of our children, the credibility of our warnings about drugs is directly related to the sincerity of our concern with fundamental human values.

The excessive use of drugs is destructive to human life. Youngsters will not believe this argument if we seem indifferent to other forms of destructiveness.

Drugs reduce the possibility of purposeful action and gradually erode the capacity for free choice. Here again, young people will doubt the sincerity of this concern if we are not alert to the ways in which freedom to make choices is already compromised. Choices are limited by prejudice, poverty, unemployment, poor education, wars. The older generation has the responsibility to show that they care about the rights of all people. When we cannot ensure these rights, we can at least side with our youngsters, doing all we can to push for change. The young need to see that we are not giving up on the democratic process, that we are involved, persistent and resilient.

Abusing drugs is a way of manipulating reality and ourselves. This is an argument that is convincing only when we demonstrate to young people that we are opposed to all ways in which one individual manipulates another or himself. They will want evidence that we do not condone treating people, even oneself, as objects to be manipulated for gain or pleasure.

The use of drugs is only one way of avoiding painful realities. Rigid sloganized thinking also diminishes our ability to face reality. It is possible to become addicted to ideas that are no longer meaningful and do not lead us toward productive solutions. Youngsters need to feel that adults can give up "addiction" to outmoded or unexamined ideas. We must join them in trying to deal with the problems in our society that trouble them keenly and to which they bring us fresh insights.

OUR RESPONSIBILITY IN PERSPECTIVE

People are civilized to the extent that they care about all the young, not just their own children. If our own children are not taking drugs, they have to see that we are deeply concerned about the children who do. Unless they have continuing evidence of this broader concern, our youngsters will conclude that our parental anxiety grows out of possessiveness and pride rather than respect for all human life.

Vast social problems cannot be solved by individuals making efforts only on behalf of themselves or their immediate families. Drug misuse is such a problem; it cannot be solved by parents improving just their own family relationships. Changes must be made to improve the quality of human life in our communities and in our society as a whole.

In spite of what is often said about the decline of parental influence, the implications of modern research are clear: parents still are a crucial force in the lives of their children. This force is not spent in the early years of childhood. It continues through adolescence and into their maturity, if we are wise enough to recognize that we can support and advise, but not program our children.

What the young do with themselves is one part of the problem; how parents influence their children is another; and equally crucial is how society supports—or fails to support—parents and their children.

All children need challenges and opportunities to develop their human potential. All adults must be concerned not only with their own children but with creating a world in which every child can live a satisfying life. The most difficult, but the most promising, solution to drug abuse is to make it possible for all young people to participate productively in a society whose aims they share.

Where to Go for Help:
Sources for Information, Counseling and Treatment

The National Clearinghouse for Drug Abuse Information is operated by the National Institute of Mental Health on behalf of the Federal agencies concerned with drug abuse. They distribute educational material upon request; they also can inform you about available facilities for counseling or treatment in or near your community. Inquiries may be addressed to:

Information
National Clearinghouse
for Drug Abuse Information
Box 1701
Washington, D.C. 20013
Telephone: (301) 496-7171

Referrals for medical and psychological treatment can be obtained through contacting your family doctor, local county and state Medical Associations and county and state Mental Health Boards.

Individual and family counseling is provided by a number of private and voluntary agencies. These include: Family Service Centers, Family Counseling Centers, Child Guidance Centers, Jewish Family Services, United Charities Associations and Catholic Charities Associations. The Family Service Association of America has 342 member agencies throughout the country. The name of the member agency nearest you may be obtained by writing to:

Family Service Association of America
44 East 23rd Street
New York, N.Y. 10010
Telephone: (212) 674-6100

A Note About The Authors...

Many members of the staff of the Child Study Association of America were involved in the preparation and writing of *You, Your Child and Drugs*. Their collaboration brings to this book a variety of professional skills as well as many years of experience in preparing mental health materials for parents. Those chiefly responsible for the writing are:

LILLIAN ERLICH, *Director of Publications, author.*
MARY HOOVER, *Member of the Board of Directors, author.*
LILLIAN OPATOSHU, *Director of Program, social work educator.*
JAMES S. OTTENBERG, *Executive Director, formerly associated with the Addiction Services Agency of New York City.*
RACHELE THOMAS, *Coordinator of Curriculum, child psychologist.*